INTRODUCING THE
PERIODIC TABLE

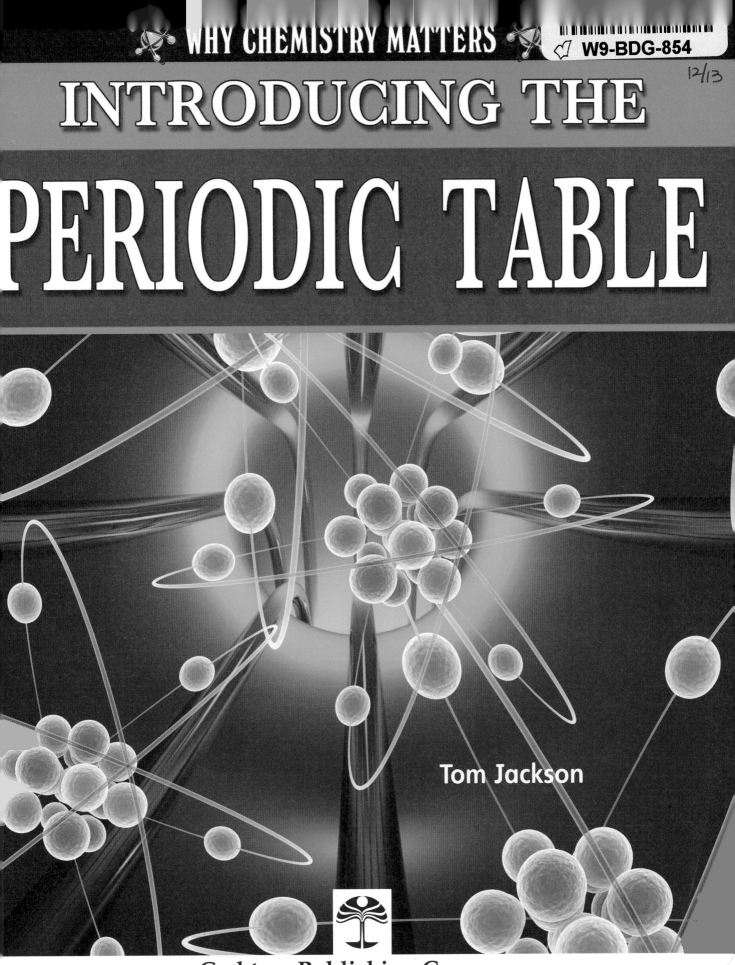

Tom Jackson

Crabtree Publishing Company

www.crabtreebooks.com

Crabtree Publishing Company
www.crabtreebooks.com

Author: Tom Jackson
Publishing plan research and development:
   Sean Charlebois, Reagan Miller
   Crabtree Publishing Company
Editor: Adrianna Morganelli
Proofreader: Crystal Sikkens
Project Coordinator: Kathy Middleton
Designer: Karen Perry
Cover Design: Samara Parent
Picture Researcher: Sophie Mortimer
Managing Editor: Tim Harris
Art Director: Jeni Child
Editorial Director: Lindsey Lowe
Children's Publisher: Anne O'Daly
Production Coordinator and
   Prepress Technician: Katherine Berti
Print Coordinator: Katherine Berti

Photographs:
Cover: Shutterstock: Michael D Brown
Interior: Edgar Fahs Smith Memorial Collection: 6;
Public Domain: 7t, D-Kuru 9, United States Nuclear
Regulatory Commission 26: **Robert Hunt Library:** 29b;
Science Photo Library: Mark A. Schneider 24;
Shutterstock: 5, 10b, 11tl, 17t, 19, 23, AG-photos 20,
Galyna Andrushko 4, Rose Armin 10t, Andrea Danti 27,
Ed Isaacs 18, Mike Ledray 22, Jeffrey Rasmussen 12b, Tena
Rebernjak 28, Carsten Reisinger 17b: **Thinkstock:**
Comstock 29t, Hemera 7b, istockphoto 11tr, 21t, 21b,
Photos.com 25, Stockbyte 11b.

All artwork and diagrams © Brown Bear Books Ltd.

Produced for Crabtree Publishing Company
by Brown Bear Books Ltd.

Library and Archives Canada Cataloguing in Publication

Jackson, Tom, 1972-
     Introducing the periodic table / Tom Jackson.

(Why chemistry matters)
Includes index.
Issued also in electronic format.
ISBN 978-0-7787-4230-2 (bound).--ISBN 978-0-7787-4234-0 (pbk.)

     1. Periodic law--Tables--Juvenile literature. 2. Chemical
elements--Juvenile literature. I. Title. II. Series: Why chemistry
matters

QD467.J33 2012   j546'.8   C2012-906385-1

Library of Congress Cataloging-in-Publication Data

CIP available at Library of Congress

**Published in
Canada
Crabtree Publishing**
616 Welland Ave.
St. Catharines, ON
L2M 5V6

**Published in the
United States
Crabtree Publishing**
PMB 59051
350 Fifth Avenue, 59th Floor
New York, New York 10118

**Published in the
United Kingdom
Crabtree Publishing**
Maritime House
Basin Road North, Hove
BN41 1WR

**Published in
Australia
Crabtree Publishing**
3 Charles Street
Coburg North
VIC, 3058

Contents

Organizing the Elements

The universe is made up of dozens of simple substances called **elements**. The **periodic** table is a chart for viewing all the elements together, so **chemists** can see very easily which ones are similar to each other and which are not.

The periodic table that is used today and seen on the wall of science labs around the world was invented in 1869. It has gotten bigger and more complicated since then, but the way in which the elements are displayed has not really changed. However, the periodic table was not the first attempt to organize the elements.

Sulfur is a yellow element found around volcanoes and hot springs.

We know today that there are 92 naturally occurring elements. These include the oxygen we breathe, the gold in jewelry, and the carbon in a lump of coal. Mostly elements are combined into more complicated substances, such as wood, carbon dioxide, or sugar. However, these can all be simplified into their ingredients of elements. What makes elements special is that they cannot be broken up into simpler ingredients. They are single, pure substances.

So hydrogen has an atomic mass of one while oxygen's is 16. The same kind of process was used by chemists to figure out true atomic masses for other elements.

Dmitri Mendeleev then saw a pattern in the list of elements. The **valence**, or combining power, of hydrogen is one—its atom can combine with just one other atom. As elements got heavier their valence went up, too. However, **periodically** the valence went back to one, and the pattern started again. Mendeleev arranged elements in rows according to this pattern, and the periodic table was born.

The early version of the periodic table was less easy to read than the one we use today. There were also a lot of gaps.

Mendeleev is said to have gotten the idea for his table while playing solitaire, a game where players arrange cards in order.

Atomic Structure

From the start, the periodic table worked well by helping chemists understand how different elements behaved. However, no one knew what it was that gave the elements their properties until the structure of atoms was discovered.

The periodic table is based on two features of the elements. First, every element has a unique atomic mass—no two weigh the same. Second, the elements with similar atomic masses fall into rough sets based on the way they combine with one another. This property is called the valence. When scientists uncovered the inner structure of atoms it showed what gave them different masses. The discovery also explained what was causing the repeating patterns seen in the periodic table.

It was once thought that nothing smaller than an atom could exist. However, early in the 20th century, it was found that atoms were made up of even smaller particles—described as subatomic particles. The first to be found was the **electron**, a tiny particle with a negative **charge**. However, atoms have no charge themselves, so scientists looked for something else inside that had a positive charge—something that would cancel out the effect of the electrons.

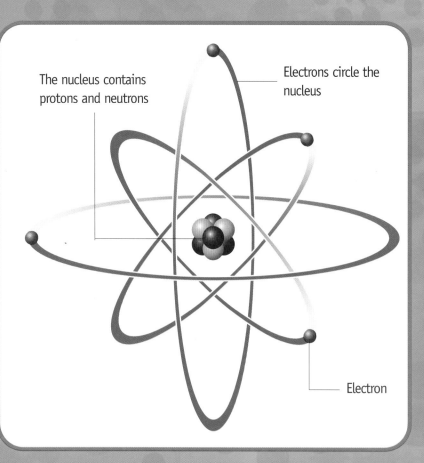

The nucleus contains protons and neutrons

Electrons circle the nucleus

Electron

An atom is mostly empty space. The **protons** and **neutrons** are gathered in the central region called the nucleus. The electrons orbit, or circle around, the nucleus.

The cathode-ray tube was used to make moving pictures on early television screens.

In 1909, scientists found that the center of the atom was made of protons. These are much heavier than electrons, but one proton still has a positive charge that is equal and opposite to the charge of one electron.

Every atom had a certain number of protons at its center, or nucleus, and an equal number of electrons moving around it. However, the atomic masses of the elements went up faster than the number of protons in their atoms. In 1932, a third subatomic particle was discovered, named the neutron. This was neutral—it had no charge—but weighed about the same as a proton and made up the missing mass inside atoms.

Cathode Rays

Electrons were discovered in cathode rays. These were strange beams formed inside a vacuum tube. The ray streamed between two electrified metal plates, creating an eerie green glow along the way. In 1899, J.J. Thomson showed that the ray was made up of tiny particles being blasted out of the metal's atoms.

Elements and Atoms

The repeating patterns that run through the periodic table can all be explained by the atomic structure of atoms. Every element has its own unique atomic structure.

An element is a substance that is made up of just one type of atom. If it were possible to change those atoms, adding or taking away protons and electrons, they would stop being atoms of one element and become atoms of an altogether different one.

Every element has a unique atomic number, which is the number of protons in the atom. For example, hydrogen has an atomic number of one—it has just one proton. Carbon has an atomic number of six, and iron's is 26. The number of electrons in an atom is always equal to the number of protons. (The number of neutrons can vary. That results in atoms of the same element existing as different versions called **isotopes**.)

The protons and neutrons form the atomic nucleus, and they give the atoms its mass. The electrons are so light that they do not really have any effect on the atomic mass. However, the way the electrons are arranged around the nucleus is what allows atoms to bond together.

Electron

Nucleus

Hydrogen has the simplest atoms and that makes the gas very lightweight. Hydrogen balloons fly higher than any other type. They are used to study the upper atmosphere.

Carbon atoms have electrons arranged in two layers. Pure carbon is found as diamonds or graphite, which is better known as pencil lead.

Nucleus

Electron

Atoms are held together by **electromagnetism**, the force behind magnets and electricity like bolts of lightning.

Chemical Bonds

Metallic bond: Outer electrons break off metal atoms. They form a "sea" of electrons that glues the atoms together, making a hard but bendy solid.

Ionic bond: An atom with only a few electrons in its outer shell gives them away. This makes it a positively charged **ion**. An atom with few empty spaces in its outer shell grabs the free electrons, forming a negative ion. The positive and negative ions are attracted to each other, making a molecule.

Covalent bond: Two or more atoms share electrons so they all have a full outer shell. The atoms connect into a molecule.

Atom

Electron

Metallic bond

Outer electron

Negative ion

Empty space

Positive ion

Molecule

Shared electrons

The black atoms in this model have a valence of four; they connect to up to four other atoms. Blue atoms have a valence of three, while the red ones have a valence of just one.

Electrons are located in layers around the nucleus. Each layer, or shell, has a maximum number of electrons it can hold, and after that a new shell forms further away from the nucleus. Atoms are most stable when their outer **electron shell** is full. They can achieve this by bonding with other atoms.

An element's valence, or number of bonds its atoms can form, depends on the number of outer electrons it has. So although he did not realize it at the time, Mendeleev's table is a way of organizing the elements according to the way their electrons are arranged.

The Modern Table

A modern periodic table is filled with information. It shows chemists the atomic structures of all the elements and indicates what kind of properties an element will have.

Every element is shown as a square on the periodic table. When Mendeleev created the first version there were just 64 elements known. That early table had a lot of empty spaces. Now there are 118 elements in it. About 90 of them are found naturally on Earth. The rest of them are made in laboratories.

The elements are known by different names in different languages. For example, iron is *fer* in French, *de hierro* in Spanish, and *tie* in Chinese.

The first people to give elements symbols were alchemists. Alchemists were like wizards; they thought they could control the elements using magic.

Match the Element to the Symbol

Most elements have letter symbols that match the way they are spelled, but others come from their Latin names. See if you can find the symbol for each of these elements.

Fe   H   Pb   Au   Cl   O

1) The symbol for oxygen
2) The symbol for hydrogen
3) Gold, known as "aurum" in Latin
4) Lead, known as "plumbum" in Latin
5) The symbol for chlorine
6) Iron, known as "ferrum" in Latin

Answers: 1 O; 2 H; 3 Au; 4 Pb; 5 Cl; 6 Fe

Elements with a few outer electrons are metals; the non-metals have large numbers of outer electrons.

To make sure everyone knows exactly which element is which, each has been given a symbol made up of one or two letters. Iron's symbol is Fe from *ferrum*, the Latin for iron.

Every element on the table is also shown with two numbers. The top one is the atomic number. This is always a whole number and shows how many protons are in the atoms of

Legend:
- ACTINIDES
- NOBLE GASES
- NON-METALS
- METALLOIDS
- HYDROGEN
- ALKALI METALS
- ALKALINE-EARTH METALS
- METALS
- LANTHANIDES

Transition metals

	Group 1	Group 2							
Period 1	1 **H** Hydrogen 1								
Period 2	3 **Li** Lithium 7	4 **Be** Beryllium 9							
Period 3	11 **Na** Sodium 23	12 **Mg** Magnesium 24							
Period 4	19 **K** Potassium 39	20 **Ca** Calcium 40	21 **Sc** Scandium 45	22 **Ti** Titanium 48	23 **V** Vanadium 51	24 **Cr** Chromium 52	25 **Mn** Manganese 55	26 **Fe** Iron 56	27 **Co** Cobalt 59
Period 5	37 **Rb** Rubidium 85	38 **Sr** Strontium 88	39 **Y** Yttrium 89	40 **Zr** Zirconium 91	41 **Nb** Niobium 93	42 **Mo** Molybdenum 96	43 **Tc** Technetium (98)	44 **Ru** Ruthenium 101	45 **Rh** Rhodium 103
Period 6	55 **Cs** Cesium 133	56 **Ba** Barium 137	Lanthanides	72 **Hf** Hafnium 179	73 **Ta** Tantalum 181	74 **W** Tungsten 184	75 **Re** Rhenium 186	76 **Os** Osmium 190	77 **Ir** Iridium 192
Period 7	87 **Fr** Francium 223	88 **Ra** Radium 226	Actinides	104 **Rf** Rutherfordium (263)	105 **Db** Dubnium (268)	106 **Sg** Seaborgium (266)	107 **Bh** Bohrium (272)	108 **Hs** Hassium (277)	109 **Mt** Meitnerium (276)

Rare-earth elements
— Lanthanides
— Actinides

57 **La** Lanthanum 39	58 **Ce** Cerium 140	59 **Pr** Praseodymium 141	60 **Nd** Neodymium 144	61 **Pm** Promethium (145)	62 **Sm** Samarium 150
89 **Ac** Actinium 227	90 **Th** Thorium 232	91 **Pa** Protactinium 231	92 **U** Uranium 238	93 **Np** Neptunium (237)	94 **Pu** Plutonium (244)

that element (and the number of electrons, too). That quantity is unique to each element. The atomic number of lithium (Li) is three. If you were to add a proton to an atom of Li, then the atomic number would become four. The atom would have changed from lithium into beryllium.

The second number, which is normally under the symbol, is the relative atomic mass (**RAM**).

This shows how heavy an atom is compared to the others. Helium has a RAM of four, which means its atom is four times heavier than a hydrogen (RAM 1) and three times lighter than a carbon atom (RAM 12). The RAM is based on the total number of particles in an atom's nucleus. Carbon has atomic number six (six protons) and a RAM of 12. Therefore it also has six neutrons (six protons + six neutrons = 12).

Periodic Table

Atomic number

Chemical symbol

| 33 |
| **As** |
| Arsenic |
| 75 |

Element name
Relative atomic mass

Group 8

Group 3	Group 4	Group 5	Group 6	Group 7	
					2 **He** Helium 4
5 **B** Boron 11	6 **C** Carbon 12	7 **N** Nitrogen 14	8 **O** Oxygen 16	9 **F** Fluorine 19	10 **Ne** Neon 20
13 **Al** Aluminum 27	14 **Si** Silicon 28	15 **P** Phosphorus 31	16 **S** Sulfur 32	17 **Cl** Chlorine 35	18 **Ar** Argon 40

28 **Ni** Nickel 59	29 **Cu** Copper 64	30 **Zn** Zinc 65	31 **Ga** Gallium 70	32 **Ge** Germanium 73	33 **As** Arsenic 75	34 **Se** Selenium 79	35 **Br** Bromine 80	36 **Kr** Krypton 84
46 **Pd** Palladium 106	47 **Ag** Silver 108	48 **Cd** Cadmium 112	49 **In** Indium 115	50 **Sn** Tin 119	51 **Sb** Antimony 122	52 **Te** Tellurium 128	53 **I** Iodine 127	54 **Xe** Xenon 131
78 **Pt** Platinum 195	79 **Au** Gold 197	80 **Hg** Mercury 201	81 **Tl** Thallium 204	82 **Pb** Lead 207	83 **Bi** Bismuth 209	84 **Po** Polonium (209)	85 **At** Astatine (210)	86 **Rn** Radon (222)
110 **Ds** Darmstadtium (281)	111 **Rg** Roentgenium (280)	112 **Cn** Copernicium (285)	113 **Uut** Ununtrium (284)	114 **Uuq** Ununquadium (289)	115 **Uup** Ununpentium (291)	116 **Uuh** Ununhexium (293)	117 **Uus** Ununseptium (295)	118 **Uuo** Ununoctium (294)

63 **Eu** Europium 152	64 **Gd** Gadolinium 157	65 **Tb** Terbium 159	66 **Dy** Dysprosium 163	67 **Ho** Holmium 165	68 **Er** Erbium 167	69 **Tm** Thulium 169	70 **Yb** Ytterbium 173	71 **Lu** Lutetium 175
95 **Am** Americium (243)	96 **Cm** Curium (247)	97 **Bk** Berkelium (247)	98 **Cf** Californium (251)	99 **Es** Einsteinium (252)	100 **Fm** Fermium (257)	101 **Md** Mendelevium (258)	102 **No** Nobelium (259)	103 **Lr** Lawrencium (260)

Periods

The rows of the periodic table are called **periods**. Each period contains the elements that have the same number of electron shells in their atoms.

There are seven periods on the periodic table. The first one contains just two elements, hydrogen and helium. These elements have the simplest atoms, made up of just one electron shell. This makes the first period unusual—the others all have a lot more than two members. The reason why period one is so small is because that first shell only has room for two electrons. When a third electron is added, making an atom of lithium, it sits as the first member of the next shell.

That makes lithium the first element in period two. This row contains many of the more familiar elements, such as carbon, nitrogen, and oxygen. It has eight members in total, which shows that there is room for eight electrons in the second shell.

As elements get heavier, their atoms arrange the electrons in larger and larger shells.

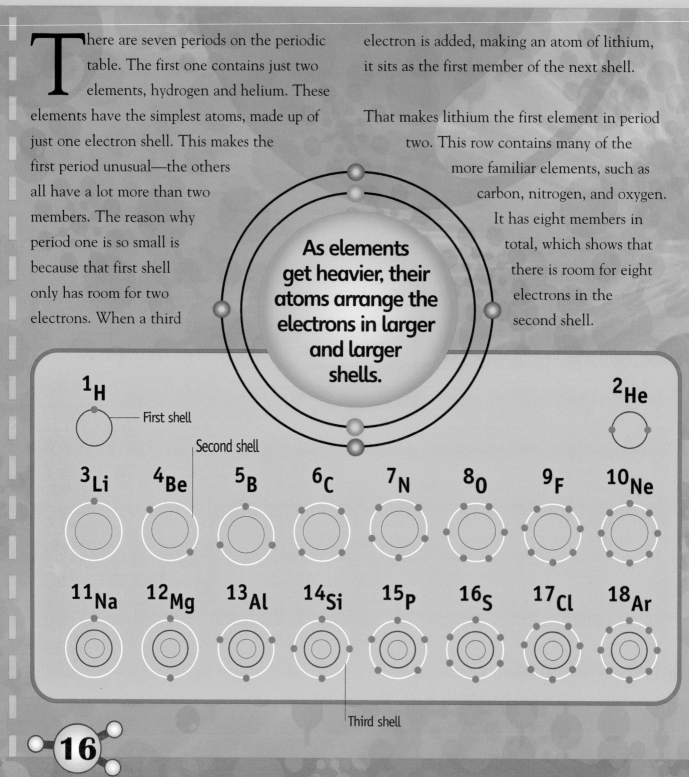

First shell

Second shell

Third shell

A neon (Ne) atom in a colored light is smaller than a lithium (Li) atom, like those in batteries, even though it weighs three times as much.

The third period also has eight members, running from sodium to argon. From period four onwards, things get more complicated as shells begin to accept larger numbers of electrons. This is what creates the central block, or **series**, in the middle of the periodic table (see page 20).

Atom Size

Even though heavier atoms contain more particles than lighter ones, atoms get smaller in size as you move along a period. There is a big gap between the nucleus and the electrons. The positive charge of the nucleus pulls the negative electrons keeping them bonded to the atom. A large nucleus (with a lot of protons) tugs on the electrons more than a small one. That pulls the electron shells closer to the nucleus, making the atom smaller.

Groups

The columns in the periodic table are called **groups**. A group contains the elements with the same number of electrons in their outermost shells.

The first group on the periodic table—Group 1—contains elements with just one electron in their outer shell. This group includes hydrogen, and metals such as sodium and potassium. Group 2 has elements with two electrons in the outer shell. It includes metals like magnesium and calcium. The system continues across the table until Group 8. This group is made up of gases that have a full set of electrons in their outer shell. (Helium is included in the group with only two electrons, but that makes a full shell also). Some chemists call this Group 0 because the elements have no outer electrons that take part in chemical bonding. As a result the group is known as the noble, or inert, gases. This means they do not react with the other elements. They have all the electrons they need to be stable.

Bicarbonate of soda, or baking soda, is a compound made from sodium and hydrogen (Group 1), carbon (Group 4), and oxygen (Group 6).

Common Salt

One of the most common substances on Earth is sodium chloride, the scientific name for table salt. This is the substance in seawater or used to season food. A molecule of salt is formed when one sodium ion bonds to a chloride ion. The ions hold onto each other very strongly making table salt a very stable substance.

This is not true of Group 1 elements, which need to just lose one electron to become stable (removing the outer shell entirely). As a result Group 1 elements, such as sodium, are very reactive and form ions easily, ready to bond to other elements. Group 7 elements (known as the halogens) are also very reactive but for the opposite reason to Group 1. They have seven electrons in the outer shell, with space for just one more to make it full. Group 7 elements, such as chlorine, tear away outer electrons from other atoms, to form stable, negatively charged ions.

Series

From the fourth period onward, the organization of the periodic table becomes more complicated. As atoms get bigger, extra electrons are added to the inside of the atom, not the outside.

The center of the periodic table is made up of a large block of elements called the transition series. *Transition* means to make a change from one thing to another, and the transition elements run between Groups 2 and 3. All the members of the set are metals, including many of the most common ones, such as copper, nickel, and iron.

Nearly all the transition elements have two electrons in the outer shells of their atoms—a few have just one. They behave in a similar way to elements in Group 2, but because they are not exactly the same they are placed in their own section.

The transition series begins with scandium, which has atomic number 21, one more than calcium. However, instead of the next electron becoming the third in the fourth outer shell (putting scandium in Group 3), it slotted in as number nine in the electron shell underneath—the atom's third shell. At this size of atom, the third shell allows more electrons in, and can hold a maximum of 18.

The Statue of Liberty is made mainly from copper, a metal in the transition series. Copper goes green when exposed to the air.

Transition metals make very colorful compounds. This amethyst crystal gets its color from manganese.

Precious Metals

There are about 30 metals in the transition series, including the so-called precious metals, gold, silver, and platinum. These metals are good for making jewelry because they are easy to polish and stay shiny.

As the atomic number goes up, and electrons are added to make the next element, the number of outer electrons stays at two—until we get to zinc. Zinc atoms have two electrons in the outer shell and 18 in the next shell—which is now full. Zinc's neighbor, gallium, has one more electron, but this sits in the outer shell, making that element a member of Group 3.

The periodic table has another series. Starting at Period 6, the atoms' inner electron shell gains room for another 14 electrons— making a maximum of 32! This series, named the rare earth elements, is shown along the bottom of the table.

Patterns in Reactivity

Understanding the way the periodic table works turns it into a powerful tool. Chemists use it as a guide to figure out how elements will react with each other and which ones are more likely to react than others.

Chemical reactions can be used to make useful substances or find out more about ones that you already have.

For one atom to bond to another one, a chemical reaction must take place. During a reaction, the atoms involved rearrange their electrons into a more stable state. This process needs energy to start. The amount of energy a reaction needs depends on how easily the atoms involved will rearrange their electrons. The most reactive elements need only a little energy to react and form bonds.

The periodic table tells which elements are more reactive than others. The elements on the left side of the table have atoms with just one or two electrons in their outer shell. They normally react by releasing their outer electrons to form charged ions. These ions then form ionic bonds.

It only requires a little energy to pull away the single outer electron from the atom in Group 1, a lithium atom, for example. A little more energy is needed to pull off the two outer electrons from a Group 2 atom, such as beryllium. Therefore Group 1 elements are more reactive than those in Group 2. This pattern continues as you move right across the table. Groups 3 and 4, in the middle of the table, are even less reactive.

However, the elements on the right side of the table are reactive too, just in a different way. The elements in Group 7, such as fluorine, have just one space left in their outer electron shells. The members of Group 6, including oxygen, have two empty spaces. These elements react by trapping the extra electrons they need to form ions. Fluorine needs less energy to trap one electron, compared to the two needed by oxygen. That makes fluorine more reactive than oxygen.

So in general, the elements to the left and right of the table are more reactive than those elements in the middle. (The exception to this are the noble gases of Group 8 [or Group 0] which have full electron shells and never really form ions or react with other elements.)

Fluorine is found in a mineral called fluorite, which glows, or fluoresces, in the dark.

Reactivity also changes as you go up and down the table. Small atoms with fewer shells hold on to their outer electrons more strongly than big ones with several shells. In large atoms, the outer electrons are further from the nucleus and so are easier to break free.

Predicting Germanium

Mendeleev said that the gaps in his table were elements that had not been discovered yet. He used his table to predict the properties of these missing elements. In 1869, he named element 32 eka-silicon and predicted that when it was found this element would be a gray, shiny solid. He also gave estimates for its melting point and density. All these were shown to be true when element 32, later re-named germanium, was finally discovered in 1886.

Therefore, elements that react by losing electrons like Group 1 are more reactive at the bottom of the table than the top.

However, on the other side of the table it works the other way around. Elements that react by trapping extra electrons, such as Group 7, are more reactive at the top of the table then at the bottom. A small fluorine atom can pull on electrons more strongly than a large iodine one and so is much more reactive. In fact fluorine and cesium are among the two most reactive elements on the table and would react with a very big explosion.

Fireworks use highly reactive elements such as lithium which makes red fireworks and sodium which makes yellow.

Reactivity Test

Use the periodic table on page 14 to arrange these sets of elements in order of reactivity, with the most reactive listed first:

1) Lithium (Li), Potassium (K), Sodium (Na)

2) Silicon (Si), Fluorine (F), Neon (Ne)

3) Magnesium (Mg), Sodium (Na) Aluminum (Al)

Answers; 1) K, Na, Li; 2) F, Si, Ne; 3) Na, Mg, Al

Radioactivity

Radioactivity is the process that makes large, unstable atoms break apart. This releases particles and **radiation** that can be dangerous to health.

In 1896, French scientist Henri Becquerel found that invisible rays were coming from a lump of rock containing uranium. These mysterious rays even came out when the rock was wrapped up in paper. It was later revealed that these rays were produced by radioactivity.

Radioactivity occurs when an atom's nucleus is so crammed full of protons and neutrons that it cannot hold onto them all.

Every so often particles are pushed out of the nucleus and released as radioactive radiation. This process is called radioactive decay. It changes the atomic number of the atom—the number of protons in the nucleus. That means radioactive atoms of one element decay into the atoms of another.

Nuclear fuel in a water tank glows blue because it releases energy as its atoms decay.

In nuclear fission one large atom is split into two smaller ones. This releases a lot of heat which is used to generate electricity.

Radioactivity is a natural process and every element from bismuth, number 83, upward is radioactive. The most common radioactive elements are uranium and thorium. Both of these can be used as fuel for generating electricity. The nuclear fuel is made to release large amounts of heat through a process called nuclear **fission**. This splits the unstable atoms in two. The heat energy is then converted into electricity.

The radiation from radioactivity is very dangerous. The fast-moving subatomic particles in it can damage living bodies, for example by burning the skin. They can even break apart important chemicals deep inside the body, causing serious illnesses, such as **cancer**.

Marie Curie

A Polish scientist named Marie Curie invented the word radioactivity. She worked in Paris with her husband Pierre at the start of the 20th century, investigating which elements were radioactive. The Curies discovered two new elements—polonium and radium. They were awarded the **Nobel prize** *for physics.*

Artificial Elements

The heaviest and most complex atom found in nature belongs to the element uranium, which has 92 protons, 92 electrons, and 146 neutrons (more or less). Scientists have been making artificial elements since the 1930s by smashing smaller atoms together so they form one larger one.

The first artificial element was made by accident. In 1936, element 43 was found in the remains left behind by one of these atom smashers. Element 43 was the last unfilled gap in the periodic table, and it appeared that this element was so radioactive that all of it had decayed out of existence long ago. There was none left in nature. Chemists called the element technetium, to reflect how it had been made by human technology. (Better testing techniques later showed that technetium was found in nature although in very small quantities.)

Technetium is a small although unusual element. Since the late 1940s, scientists have been making atoms larger than uranium, which definitely do not exist in nature. They include plutonium made in nuclear power plants. Most are made in bigger and better atom smashers, or particle accelerators. Many of the new elements are named after famous scientists.

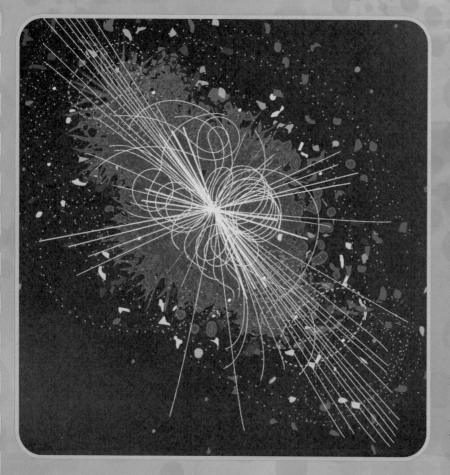

Scientists smash atoms and other small particles together at enormous speeds and watch to see what happens. That tells them what the universe was like billions of years ago.

Americium is named for America. Other elements are named for places, such as californium (California) and francium (France).

For example there are curium (96), einsteinium (99), mendelevium (101), and seaborgium (106). This last one was named after Glenn Seaborg in 1997, who discovered it and several other artificial elements.

Seaborgium was named for Glenn Seaborg, the only person to have an element named after him while he was still alive.

Smoke Detectors

Artificial elements are not just found in high-tech laboratories. Most houses will have tiny amounts of the artificial element americium inside smoke detectors. A tiny sample of this element produces very small—and completely safe—amounts of radiation. Normally the radiation just streams across a gap in the heart of the smoke alarm, toward a detector. However, when smoke gets inside, even a tiny amount will block the radiation, and the alarm goes off.

Glossary

atom The smallest unit of an element

atomic mass A measure of how heavy the atoms of an element are compared to the atoms of other elements; also known as RAM

cancer A disease that makes the body grow damaging lumps; cancer can be caused by radioactive radiation

cathode ray A beam of electrons that runs between two electrified metal plates. Old-fashioned televisions have cathode rays.

charge The property of ions and some subatomic particles; objects with an overall negative charge attract objects with a positive charge. Things with the same charge push each other away.

chemist A scientist who studies the elements and figures out how substances are formed from combinations of atoms

covalent A chemical bond where atoms sit next to each other, sharing their outer electrons

electromagnetism The force that acts between charged particles, making them attract or repel each other

electron A tiny negatively charged particle that is found in atoms

electron shell One of the layers in which electrons are arranged around the outside of an atom

element A simple natural substance that cannot be simplified into any other ingredients

fission Where an object splits apart

gas The state of matter where a substance is made up of small units that move independently of each other in all directions; steam is the gas form of water

group A column in the periodic table

ion A charged particle that is formed when an atom loses or gains one or more electrons

isotope A version of an atom that has a certain number of neutrons

metal An element that is a hard and shiny solid; metal elements have atoms with only a few outer electrons

metallic To do with metals

molecule A combination of atoms that are arranged in a certain way

neutron A subatomic particle with no charge

Nobel prize An international science prize named for Alfred Nobel, the inventor of dynamite

non-metal An element that is not a metal; non-metal atoms have a lot of electrons in their outer shells

period A row in the periodic table

periodic When something repeats in a pattern

periodically Something that happens every so often

proton A subatomic particle with a positive charge

radiation The high-energy particles and beams released by radioactive elements. A completely different form of radiation includes light, heat, and radio waves.

RAM Stands for relative atomic mass

series A section of the periodic table containing elements that have free spaces in their inner electron shells

valence Combining power, a measure of how many bonds an atom can form at the same time

Index

Web Finder

http://education.jlab.org/itselemental/index.html

www.bayerus.com/msms/MSMS_Science_Fun/
    PeriodicTable/PeriodicTable.aspx

www.chemtutor.com/perich.htm#top

http://periodictable.com/